When Time Began

Rhona Pipe

Illustrated by
Jenny Press

OLIVER
NELSON

THOMAS NELSON PUBLISHERS
Nashville • Atlanta • London • Vancouver

When time began,
God made the earth.
It had no life.
It had no shape.
It was boiling and black.
And God's Spirit moved
over the earth.

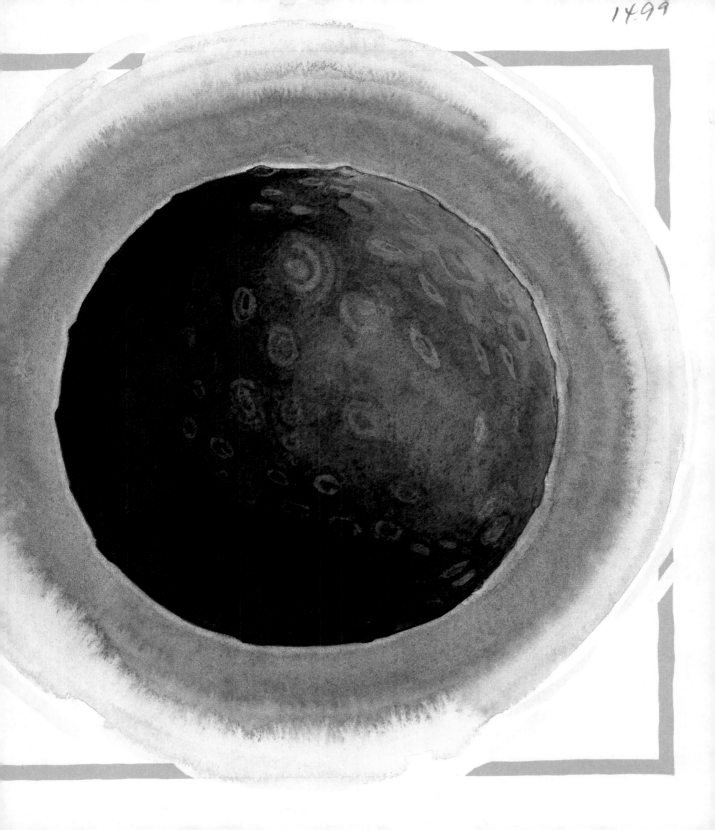

God said,
"Let there be light."
And light came.
God was glad
when He saw the light.
He named the light *day*.
And He named
the darkness *night*.
That was Day One in the
making of the earth.

Then God said,
"Let there be a roof over the earth.
Let it keep some waters
above the earth.
Let it keep some waters
on the earth."
And it was done.
God named the roof *sky*.
That was Day Two in the making
of the earth.

Then God said,
"Let the waters come together.
Let there be dry land."
And it was done.
God named the waters *seas*
and the land *earth*.
God was glad when He saw
the seas and the earth.

Then God said,
"Let plants with seeds grow
on the earth.
Let trees with fruit grow
on the earth."
And it was done.
God was glad when He saw the
plants and trees.
That was Day Three in the
making of the earth.

Then God said,
"Let lights come in the sky.
Let the lights shine down
on the earth."
And it was done.
God made the sun for the day.
God made the moon and stars
for the night.
He was glad
when He saw the lights.
That was Day Four in the
making of the earth.

Then God said,
"Let fish fill the seas.
Let birds fly in the sky."
And it was done.
God was glad when He saw the fish.
God was glad when He saw the birds.
He said, "Be happy
and grow in number."
That was Day Five in the
making of the earth.

Then God said,
"Let animals live on the earth.
Let the animals be big and small."
And it was done.
And God was glad when He saw
the animals.

Last of all God said,
"Now We will make people.
We will make men and
women like Us.
They will look after the fish
and the birds.
They will look after the animals
on the earth." And it was done.
And God said, "Be happy and
grow in number. You have
grain and fruit to eat."

God looked at what He had made.

It was very good.

He was glad.

That was the end of Day Six.

It was the end of making the earth.

God did not work on Day Seven.

He said, "Day Seven is a happy day.

It is a day to rest.

It is a day to praise Me."

Noah's Story

Halcyon Backhouse

Illustrated by
Jenny Press

God was very sad.
The people He had made
chose to hate Him.
On top of that,
they hated each other.
Only Noah was good.

God spoke to Noah.
"I will end these people.
Make a ship out of good timber."
Noah cut some trees.
His three sons helped him.

God told Noah how to make the ship.

It was very big.

It had three decks and a roof.

It had a lot of rooms.

All the people made fun of Noah.

"You are crazy," they said.

"Where is the water?"

God said,
"Get seven pairs of
all clean animals.
Get one pair of
all unclean animals.
Take them all on the boat.
Get plenty of food."
And Noah did what God said.
"What is that crazy Noah up to?"
the people asked.

Noah went into the ship.
He took his wife.
He took his sons
and their wives.
And God shut the door.
Then the wind came up.
The wind blew clouds
across the sky.
Drops of rain began to fall.
But Noah was safe.

The rain fell.

It made pools on the ground.

The pools became lakes.

The lakes became a sea.

And the ship floated on the sea.

The sea was gray.

The sky was gray.

And the rain fell.

The rain fell for forty days.

But God did not forget Noah.
One day, the rain stopped.
After a long time
the water went down.
And the boat got stuck on a mountain.
Noah sent out a raven.
He never saw it again.

Then Noah sent out a dove.
It did not find a place to rest.
So it came back.
After a week he sent it out again.
All day he waited.

The dove came back with a leaf
in its beak.
At last the flood had gone!

Noah waited one more week.
Then he sent the dove out again.
The dove found a home on land.
It did not come back.
So Noah took off the roof
and looked out.
He saw thick mud.
It was wonderful.

God said, "You can all get out now."
God put a rainbow in the sky.
He said, "This rainbow is My promise.
I will not flood the world again."
And Noah and his family praised God.

Samson the Strong Man

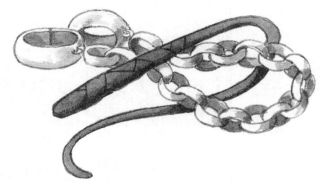

Rhona Pipe

Illustrated by
Jenny Press

"The sea people are coming.
Quick! Hide!
They want our food and sheep.
They want to kill us!"
God's people were scared
of the sea people.

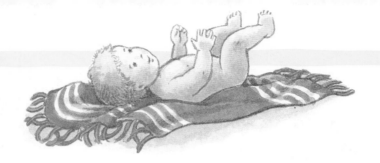

Manoah's wife was sad.
She did not have a child.
One day God sent an angel to her.
"God will give you a son,"
the angel said.
"Your son will help to set
your people free.
He will belong to God.
Do not cut his hair."

Samson grew up very strong.
Once he killed a lion
with his bare hands!
One day he lost his temper.
He killed a lot of sea people.
He began a war.
The sea people were scared
of Samson.

The sea people wanted to kill Samson.
But Samson was too strong.
Then Samson fell in love
with Delilah.
"Find out what makes
Samson strong,"
the sea people said.
"We will pay you well, Delilah."

"Samson, what could make you weak?"
Delilah asked.
"Tie me up with seven new strings,"
Samson joked.
Wrong.
"Don't tease me,"
Delilah said.
"What will make you weak?"
"Tie me with brand new ropes."
Wrong.

"Come on," Delilah said.
"Tell me."
"Weave seven strands of my
hair in your loom."
Wrong.
"If you love me, then tell me.
Tell me!" Samson gave in.
"My long hair shows I trust God,"
he said.
Delilah told the sea people
Samson's secret.

Samson fell asleep.

His head was on Delilah's lap.

The sea people cut off his hair.

"Samson! Samson!

The sea people are here!"

Delilah said.

Samson woke up and said,

"I will get free all right."

But Samson did not know

God had left him.

He was weak.

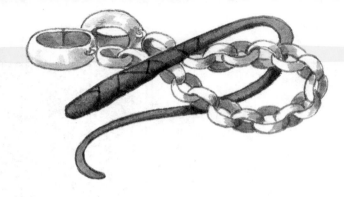

The sea people got Samson.
They put him in chains.
They put out his eyes.
They made blind Samson walk
round and round.
He had to pull a rope to grind corn.
His hair began to grow out.
And Samson cried to God for help.

The sea people held a party
for their god.
They got Samson and made him
do tricks for them.
Two posts held up the temple.
Samson stood between them.
"God, make me strong again,"
Samson prayed. "Then let me die."
And he pushed the posts.

Down came the posts.
Down came the temple.
Down came all the sea people.
All their leaders were killed.
And Samson died happy.
He had trusted God again.
He had helped to set
his people free.

David and Goliath

Halcyon Backhouse

Illustrated by
Stephen Walsh

When David was a boy, he had a job.
He looked after his dad's sheep.
Lions and bears were in the hills.
But David was a good shot
with his sling.
And God helped him keep
the sheep safe.

The country was at war.
And the enemy was close
to David's farm.
David had three big brothers.
They went off to fight
for King Saul.

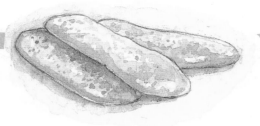

David's dad said,
"Take this bread and cheese
to your brothers.
See how they are getting
along in the army."

Goliath came out from
the enemy lines.
He was a giant.
He was over nine feet tall.
He yelled out,
"Pick a man to fight me.
Go on! I dare you!
The one who wins,
wins the war!"

"Oh — er — help!"
said King Saul's men.
"We are in big trouble!"

But David said,
"God is on our side.
What is the reward
if we kill that man?
He does not love God."

David's brother said,
"You pest! Why are you here?
Run home to your sheep."

"I just asked!" David said.
And he went to find King Saul.

"I will fight the giant for you,"
David said.
"And I will kill him."

"How can you?" asked Saul.
"You are just a kid."

"To God, Goliath is nothing,"
said David.
"God saved me from lions and bears.
He will save me from Goliath, too."

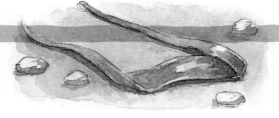

"All right," said Saul.
"You give it a try.
And God go with you."
Saul gave David his
armor and sword.
But they were far too big
for David.

So David did not use them.
He had his stick and his sling.
And he had his trust in God.

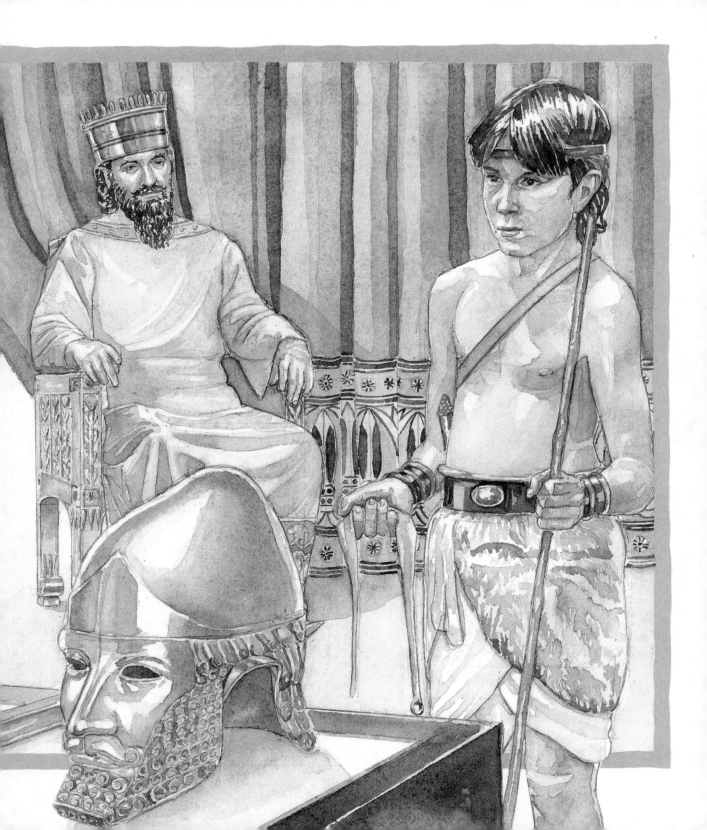

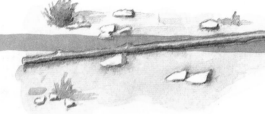

"Ha! Ha!" said Goliath.
"What is that stick for? A dog?
Ha! Ha! Come on,
I will make mush out of you.
Baby face!"

David put a stone in his sling.

Round and round went the sling.
Then zing! Out flew the stone
— and — crash!
Down fell Goliath.
David had won.

"Now the whole world knows.
God saves the people who trust Him,"
David said.

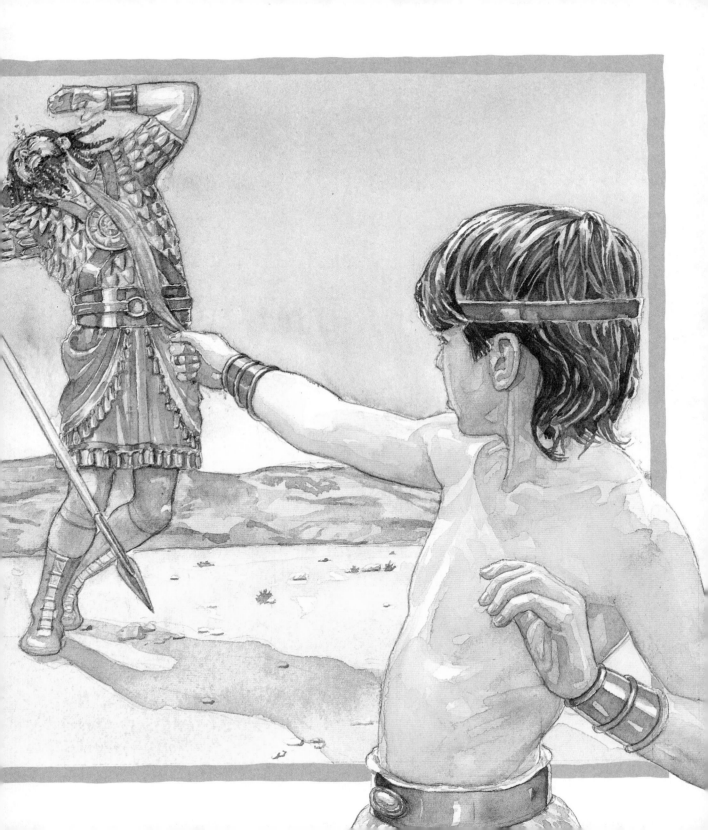

Daniel and the Lions' Den

Rhona Pipe

Illustrated by
Annabel Spenceley

"Daniel is the best man I have,"
said the king.
"I trust him.
I will make him my
prime minister."

This made the top men
in the kingdom mad.

"We do not want Daniel to boss us,"
they said.
"It is time to get rid of him.
Make a list of all the
bad things he does.
Give the list to the king."
Did the plan work? No!
Daniel did not do bad things.
"We will try plan B,"
they said.

The top men went to the king.
"O great king," they said.
"O king, may you live a long time.
Make a law that people must pray
only to you.
Anyone who breaks the law
will be thrown to the lions."
"What a good idea!"
the king said.

As soon as the law was passed,
Daniel went home.
He went upstairs and prayed to God.
He prayed by the window
as he always did.

The top men rushed to the king.
"O great king," they said.
"What a bad thing!
Daniel is praying.
And not to you!
To the lions with him!"
Then the king saw that he
had been tricked.
But it was too late.

All day long the king
did his best to think.
He tried to find a way
to save Daniel.
At the end of the day
the top men came back.
"You cannot break one
of your own laws,"
they said.
"Very well," said the king.
"Take Daniel to the lions' pit."

The king went to see Daniel.
"I am sorry," he said.
"Maybe your God will save you."
They let Daniel down into the pit
full of lions.
They put a stone over the mouth
of the pit.
The stone had the king's seal.

The king went back to
his palace.
He was too upset
to eat or drink.
He stayed awake all night.
He thought about the lions
and Daniel.

When the sun came up,
the king went to the pit.
"Daniel," he called.
"Has your God saved you?"
And Daniel called back,
"O king, may you live a long time.
My God sent an angel.
The angel closed the mouths
of the lions.
I am not hurt at all."

The king was happy.
"Pull Daniel out!" he said.
"And throw all my top men in."
Then the king sent out a letter.
It said: Daniel's God is the true God.
He is a God who saves those
who trust Him.
I am making a new law.
Everyone is to pray to Daniel's God.

The Shepherd's Story

Halcyon Backhouse

Illustrated by
Annabel Spenceley

I will not forget that night.
We had lit a fire
to keep our sheep safe.
Wolves are scared of fire.
Soon we were scared, too,
but not of the fire.

We sat and we talked.
Then we saw a bright light.
And in the light was an angel!
I went hot and cold.
I felt sick.
Then the angel spoke.

"Do not be scared," he said.
His voice was like music.
"I have good news.
Your King has been born.
You will find Him
in King David's town.
He is in a manger."
"What!" I said.
"He is where animals eat?"

Then the sky was full of angels.
Lots of them.
And they were singing.
"Glory to God," they said.
"And peace on earth to those
God is pleased with."

Then the angels went away.
And there were just us
and the sheep.
I said, "Let us go to town.
Let us see what God has
told us about."

The town was crowded.
"Let us try the inn," I said.
"Try the stable," someone said.
"The stable!" I said.
"What sort of place is that
for a baby King?"

But there He was,
just like the angel had said.
He was asleep.
We stood outside.
We did not go in.
It did not seem right.

"Come on in,"
His mother said.
She smiled at us.
And we all began to talk
at the same time.

After that we told
the story to everyone
we met.
Some people said
we were crazy.
But we did not care.
"Praise God!" we kept saying.
"God is great."

Then we went back to the sheep.
God had kept them safe.
Now I think about that angel
and the baby.
The King has come!
Hurrah!
I cannot wait till He grows up.

Martha and Mary

Halcyon Backhouse

Illustrated by
Jenny Press

No one moved in the streets.
The village by the hill
was quiet.
A dog slept in the sun.
The women sewed and cooked
in the shade.

All of a sudden
there was a noise.

"Did you hear that?"
Mary asked her sister Martha.
"I am sure there was a noise.
I will find out what it was."

"Come quick," Mary said.
"It is Jesus and His friends.
There is a crowd.
Let us invite them for a meal.
You ask Him, Martha.
You are the oldest."

"Jesus!" Martha said.
"You did not tell us You were coming.
It is good to see You again.
Will you come for a meal . . .
er . . . all of you?"

Martha was thrilled.
But she was upset, too.

There was so much to do.
First she had to buy more food.
And wash it.
And cook it.
And bake bread.
And put it all out.
And pour drinks.

No. First she would go to the well.
She would get more water.
Jesus and His friends had to wash.
She would get lots of towels
from somewhere.

Then she would get more cups
and plates and . . .
Martha needed help.
Where was Mary?

Mary was with Jesus.
She sat on the ground with
the others.
Mary wanted to hear Jesus.

Martha felt like crying.
She said, "Jesus, do You
care about me?
I have all this work to do.
All by myself.
It is not fair.
Tell Mary she must help."

Jesus looked at Martha.

He smiled. "Oh, Martha," He said.

"You worry too much.

You put the wrong things first.

Only one thing is important.

And Mary has it right."

What do you think Martha did then?

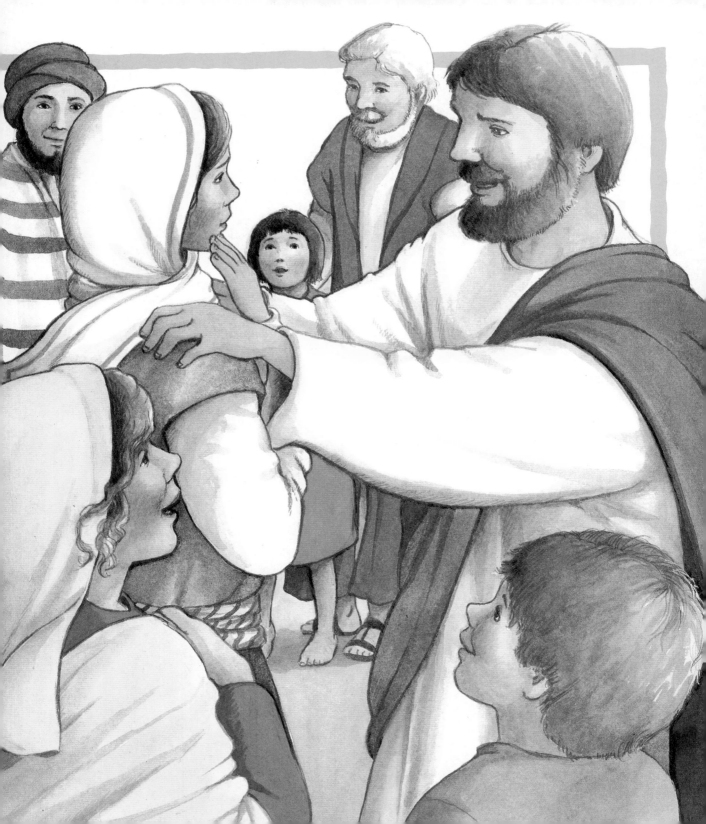

The Easter Story

Rhona Pipe

Illustrated by
Annabel Spenceley

"Oh, no!" Mary of Magdala said
to her two friends.
"We forgot about that stone
in front of the cave.
It is too big for us to move.
What will we do?"

Jesus had died three days ago.
It was Sunday morning.
The sun was rising.
Mary and her friends had come
to the garden.
They had sweet oils to rub on
Jesus' dead body.
But now they were stuck.

But wait a minute …
"Look!" Mary said.
"The stone has been moved!
Now what has happened?"
The three friends crept to the tomb.
They went into the black mouth
of the cave.

A young man sat on the stone shelf.

He wore bright white clothes.

The women stood still.

They were too scared to speak.

"Do not be scared," the man said.
"Jesus is not here. He is alive.
Look. His body is gone.
Go and tell His friends."
Mary thought he was lying.
She thought the man had taken
Jesus' body.
She did not know the man
was an angel.

Mary raced out of the garden.
She ran to Peter and John.
"They have taken Jesus' body,"
she said.
"We do not know where it is."
Peter and John ran to the cave.

Slowly Mary went back.

No one was there.

She stood outside the cave.

She cried.

She bent down and looked in.

Two men were in the cave.

"Why are you crying?"
they asked.
"They have taken Jesus' body,"
she said.
Just then there was a noise
behind her.

She turned around.
A man stood in the garden.
"Why are you crying?"
he asked.
"Who are you looking for?"
Mary thought he was the gardener.
She said, "If you took the body, sir,
please tell me.
I will go and get it."

The man said, "Mary!"
His voice was full of love.
Only one man said Mary's name
that way.
Jesus! It was Jesus.
Alive.
"My Teacher!" Mary said.
She was very, very happy.
"Tell all My friends," Jesus said.